4 S's of A

Committed Leader

by

DEWAYNE FREEMAN

Foreword by Dr. Samuel Chand
Special Note from Dr. Steve Houpe

To Rev. Bruce Hyman
Dewayne Freeman

PRAISE FOR THE 4 S's OF A COMMITTED LEADER AND AUTHOR DEWAYNE FREEMAN

What a great privilege of friendship I have in knowing Dewayne Freeman. Pastor Freeman possesses a selfless zeal for helping others become successful according to Biblical truths. His teachings seek to edify believers with key principles such as seeing, submitting, serving and sowing right—all of which must be motivated by a love for God. Pastor Freeman is committed to helping readers of all ages understand the correlating relationship that exists between faithfully implementing such truths, and living the abundant life that God ordained for His people. Through relevant Scriptural references, he succinctly points out the road map for us to enjoy God's best! This inspiring guidepost will help you to realize your full potential and is simply a must-read for anyone seeking to bear tangible fruit of betterment and growth.

What a blessing this great servant is to the world. It's just amazing how this anointed vessel is used of God! May the truth in this book transform your thinking—because when you change your thinking, you change your life!

I am delighted to recommend this authentic, passionate book, "4 S's of A Committed Leader," by my dear friend Dr. Dewayne Freeman. We have ministered together over the years and the principles and convictions that I have watched him live by have made him one of the most influential and effective men of God on the East Coast. Enjoy!!!

Dr. Steve Houpe
Harvest Church

4 S's of A

Committed Leader

by

DEWAYNE FREEMAN

Foreword by Dr. Samuel Chand
Special Note from Dr. Steve Houpe

4 S's of A Committed Leader

ISBN: 978-0-9828180-4-6

Freeman Publishing
c/o Spirit of Faith Christian Center
2261 Oxon Run Drive
Temple Hills, Maryland 20748

www.FreemanPublishing.info

DEDICATION

This book is dedicated to my dad, Robert O. Freeman, who modeled before me the principles of commitment discussed herein and to my wife Anjelisa "Lisa" Freeman, my cheerleader, supporter and assistant in helping me fulfill my God given assignment. This book is also dedicated to all of those who will read it and commit to change, which will help me keep my vow to God, that when I leave the presence of His people, physically or through words on a page, they will be better equipped than they were before coming in contact with me.

FOREWORD

Some books inform, others inspire and instruct; however, the book you hold in your hands does all that and more.

In "The 4 S's of a Committed Leader," my friend Pastor Dewayne Freeman breaks down into bite-sized pieces what it means to be a committed leader. Not just committed. Not just a leader. But a committed leader—the true heart and the function.

The pathway is not to simply see, submit, serve and sow, but to do those things with the right heart and the right attitude.

In my years of ministry leadership, I have personally experienced deficits in all of the above in my own life. Often I could see, but not submit. Sometimes I have served without submitting. "The 4 S's of a Committed Leader" brings a tangible balance in all things. These four principles are like the four bases in baseball—you have to touch all four for the run to be counted. Missing any of them negates the hit.

Pastor Dewayne Freeman is the coach standing on the sidelines, making sure you touch all bases.

This book will remind you that your life counts. You'll not only read this book, but recommend it to others.

Samuel R. Chand

Dr. Samuel R. Chand

x

TABLE OF CONTENTS

INTRODUCTION

"The 4 S's of Committed Leadership," was written to assist people, especially Christians, who aspire to fully embrace the leadership qualities that God has given them. When applied, the principles discussed in this book will cause increase and promotion to be evident in your Christian walk, your church and in every area of your life. My vow to God is that when I leave the presence of His people—physically or through words on a page—they will be better equipped than before coming into contact with me. This book is part of my commitment and faithfulness to that vow. Many people are not concerned with making a difference in the lives of others; I am not one of them.

Most pastors and leaders are looking for committed people to help carry the vision that God has placed in their hearts. Generally, pastors and leaders have enough people in their churches and/or organizations to get things done. The challenge is the shortage of committed people who will see the vision through to completion. My purpose is to teach you through my life how to support the vision of the man or woman God has placed in your life. Get a hold of this: it doesn't matter who you are serving (your pastor, minister, family, boss) or whether you are serving them at home, at your job or at your church. If you keep these 4 S's in mind, you will have more success in every area of your life. This I know from experience and from studying the Word of God.

There are things that people "quote" from the Bible that when you study for yourself, you find aren't even there. We've all heard people quote the "scripture," 'God won't put more on you than you can bear.' That is not in the Bible. We should be glad it's not, otherwise we would have to stop asking Him to shower us with blessings until they overtake us? We are steadily praying, 'bless me Lord until it overtakes me. I want that pressed down, running over blessing like in Luke 6:38.' Hold on, I thought you said, 'He won't put more on you than you can bear.' Isn't overtaking someone more than they can bear? God will bless you more than you can bear to make you an example of His goodness for others; and so you can be a blessing to somebody else.

2 Timothy 2:15: *15Study to shew thyself approved unto God, a workman that needeth not to be ashamed, rightly dividing the word of truth.*

For a clear understanding of our purpose and potential, we must read and study our instruction manual, the Bible, rather than trying to figure it out on our own or taking someone else's word as truth. We should always read the Word of God with fresh eyes to avoid seeing through the eyes of our old way of thinking. Otherwise, we will never fully understand what the scripture is talking about, or how to apply it to our lives. John 8:32: *32And ye shall know the truth, and the truth shall make you free.*

The scripture doesn't say the truth will *set* you free, it says the truth will *make* you free. If you're set free, you can be bound again. When you are made free, you are free indeed. It's the truth that you know and are experiencing in your life that will make you free. (You can be like me, a Free-man. Get it? My name is Freeman. It's OK to laugh sometimes!) Evidently, if you listen to Jesus, who we know from scripture is a man who did not lie and does as He says, you will be made free. Conversely, if you listen to the lies of the enemy, your life will be one of bondage.

Understand there are three components that you will not find in a lie:

1. **Purpose** – an understanding of why a thing exists

2. **Potential** – an understanding of what a thing can do

3. **Principle** – an understanding of how a thing functions.

These components tell you the why, what and how of truth. If you violate these principles, you compromise the integrity of truth and will never fully experience the purpose of the thing. For instance, most men, when faced with having to assemble furniture, toys, bicycles, etc... tend to open the box, set the instructions aside and start putting the thing together based on the picture, attempting to figure it out as they go along. A few years ago, I bought a vacuum cleaner. After spending a lot of time trying to put it together, I decided to use the instructions. An amazing thing happened. With every instruction I followed, more of the potential of the vacuum cleaner was revealed. The final instructions were to put the plug into the electrical socket, flip the switch and the machine would come on. All I had to do was follow the instructions to release the power and potential of the vacuum machine. There was also a label that said, 'do not put this machine in water.' The message was, if you violate this principle, you compromise the potential of the vacuum cleaner and may never fully experience its purpose. Just like when we do not follow the instructions and principles in the Word of God, we will not fully release our God-given power and potential.

People have been saying for the longest time that Jesus is coming back for a church without a spot or a wrinkle. That ain't even in the Bible and I'm glad that it ain't! (Yes, I said ain't.) If that was the case, He would never come back. That idea is misunderstood from Ephesians 5:27, which reads: [27]That he might present it to himself a glorious church, not having a spot, or wrinkle, or any such thing; but that it should be holy and without blemish.

In that verse, there is nothing about 'coming back,' it says that He might present it to Himself a glorious church not having spot or wrinkle or any such thing, but that it should be holy and without blemish. Unfortunately, the church has misquoted that scripture for centuries. Surely, neglecting to tithe is a spot. If it isn't a spot, it certainly is a wrinkle and we know that many folks are not tithing. If fornication is not a wrinkle, surely it's a spot and there are people in the pulpit and in the pews who are guilty. If we have to wait for everybody to tithe, stop fornicating, backbiting and lying before Jesus comes back, He will never come back. Study the Word of God for yourself so that you will See Right, so that you can Submit Right, and then Serve Right and Sow Right. As a result, you will experience increase and promotion like never before. Oh, and another 'S' – you will Soar Right too. This book will help you to become that committed leader that the Body of Christ needs.

CHAPTER 1 - SEE RIGHT

We have all heard it said that 'eyes that look are common, but eyes that see, are rare.' We all look at things. Young children point and say, look at that dog, or light or something. But the word "see" refers to your perception; what you see beyond what you're looking at. To see right, means you must perceive right. How we perceive what we see will determine what we receive.

In the natural, if someone was pointing their finger or an object toward your eyes, you would attempt to cover them to avoid physical injury. As a leader, you must do the same; protect your spiritual eyes since your perception has a direct impact on your future actions. The devil is after your seeing, your perception. He knows that where there is no vision, the people perish (Proverbs 29:18). What do you think he was after with Samson, the strongest man in the world, as recounted in Judges 16? The devil used people to set a trap for him and when they caught him, the first thing they did was put out his eyes—to steal his vision. God uses common vision to connect people. The devil wants to break your connection by damaging your vision so you will easily walk away from those connections. To be a committed leader, you must see right.

Some people come to their pastor seeing only the problems, yet cannot or choose not to see a solution. Whether you perceive the challenge as a problem or an opportunity will determine how you address the situation, since your perception is your reality. Pastors and leaders need people to see past the problems and offer solutions.

Perception is a powerful, powerful thing. It does not matter if it is reality to anyone else. What you perceive may or may not be accurate, but because it is true to you, it dictates your response. It bears repeating, **perception is everything.**

How you perceive a person will determine what you receive from that person. That's true even with God Himself. He wants to give you everything that He has, but your perception will determine what you receive. You say everyone else is rich because that's what you see. If you cannot see it for yourself, you will never be able to experience it. You will never live it. You have to see yourself on top and blessed. Even if the whole world is against you, seek God with all of your heart. If God be for you, He is greater than the whole of the world against you. Your perception has to be changed and you are the only one who can change it. It's your choice.

The children of Israel could not go into the Promised Land because of their perception of the spies. When they returned from scouting out the land, they reported that there were giants in the land and they saw the Israelites as grasshoppers. The giants didn't even see the spies, let alone talk to them. How did they know what they were thinking? They didn't. It was the perception of the spies that stopped the Israelites from going into the land that flowed with milk and honey. Their perception became not just their reality, but also that of all the Israelites. Their experience fed into the perception that they were like grasshoppers in their sight and nothing that Joshua and Caleb said would change it. Your perception will even override the truth that is right in front of you.

Your perception will either minimize or maximize a person's role in your life. The devil does not want you to perceive properly. God will connect you to someone to take you to the next level as His representative; sent specifically to help you. God can send someone into your life, but if you are not seeing right, you will not even know that God sent them specifically for you. The person you are supposed to value has become the person you treat like trash. For example, when God gave you parents, His plan was that they would guide you through life. When you dishonor your parents, you dishonor God and your days will not be long on the earth (Exodus 20:12). How you perceive your parents will determine what you receive from them.

Of equal importance, we should never allow anybody to talk negatively about our pastors. You must raise a standard whereby people will not bring you their trash. If anyone comes to you talking trash, it is an indication that you have become his or her own personal trash can.   Do not allow other people to negatively affect your life with their perceptions.

I believe with all my heart, that God designed our lives to be fewer than three people away from anything we want or need. The challenge is that the enemy has sent people to hook up with us that God never intended for us to be in relationship with. They are pouring into our lives, causing us not to see right. Remember, good eyes come from good ears. You cannot just allow anybody to speak into your life.

Watch the friends you hang around and the conversations they have around you.

God puts us in an environment for our growth, yet sometimes we do not grow because of past experiences and negative relationships. Likewise, God will lead you to a church, but because you were hurt before, you will not receive from the pastor. He put you in a place with a man and/or woman of God to help you to move forward, and you cannot see it because of the pain of your past. You must change your perception and move forward in the things of God. Your perception is your reality; how you perceive a person will determine what you will receive from that person.

Some women are single, and will stay single, until they start to see right. They have had so many negative experiences with men and their perception is damaged, so they can't see the good man standing right in front of them. Some marital relationships are not successful because of their perception of one another. Before saying 'I do,' the wife never let the husband see her unless she was all dressed up, making the best impression. He would never let her open a car door and would stay on the phone with her all night, making a good impression. As soon as they said, 'I do,' something happened. Now that they're married, she's comfortable running around with a rag on her head, and he won't open a car door for her when her hands are full. Why? Their perceptions have shifted. They are no longer concerned with how the other person sees them. Remember, how you see a person has a direct impact on your actions toward that person.

Matthew 13:57: *57 And they were offended in him. But Jesus said unto them, A prophet is not without honour, save in his own country, and in his own house.*

Jesus wanted to do great and mighty works in the lives of the people in His hometown, however he was severely limited by their perception. This is Jesus!— the Son of the Living God—and they didn't see Him right. At certain times, even Jesus checked the perception of His disciples. He asked, "Who do men say I am?" knowing that how they perceived Him would minimize or maximize His role in their lives. God sent his only begotten son into this world to save all of us, yet some did not see him as a Savior. They did not see him as the Messiah, and as a result, they could not receive from him. They answered, 'some say you are this, some say you are that.' Then Jesus asked, "Who do you say I am?" Peter said, "Thou art the Christ, the son of the living God" (Matthew 16:16). Jesus told Peter that he perceived properly based on what the Holy Spirit revealed to Him. Where did your perception of your pastor or leader come from? If your perception was not given by God, and you're not sure of it, their impact in your life will be minimized.

Can you imagine being David, a leader at Saul's church? In 1 Samuel 18, Saul came back from a battle having killed 1,000 of the enemy. David killed 10,000. While at Saul's victory party, Saul pulled out his javelin and threw it at David! If David had not moved, that javelin would have stuck him to the wall. (OK, at least it would have injured him.) Even with that, David did not change his perception of Saul. Maybe David thought Saul did that because he was drunk. Then Saul did it again! Still David maintained his perception and honor for Saul as God's anointed. If you were in David's shoes, would you have continued to perceive Saul as being anointed by God?

The book of John, Chapter 4, tells the story of a woman being in the right place with the wrong perception, just like many of us. This particular woman came to the well at a time when she knew nobody would be there, because she was the talk of the town and wanted to avoid the drama. As she approached, she saw a man sitting on the well. When she got there, Jesus said to her, "Give me something to drink." She looked at Jesus and said, 'Excuse me? You have been sitting here all this time and when I get here you ask me to give you something to drink?' Her perception was jacked up. She went on to remind him that she was a Samaritan and He was a Jew and should not be talking to her anyway. Jesus told her, 'if you knew who I was, you would be asking me for something to drink.' She had Jesus sitting right in front of her, yet she did not perceive Him. When you don't see right, you don't act right.

Then He asked about her husband. The woman answered and said, "I have no husband." Jesus said, "thou has well said I have no husband for thou has had five husbands and he whom thou hast now is not thou husband." What Jesus was saying was 'girl, you shacking.' She replied, "Sir, I perceive that thou art a prophet" (John 4:19). Notice, her perception changed and she started seeing right. She had Jesus in front of her all the time, yet she could not perceive him as a prophet until He spoke words that allowed her to see right. The truth that she heard helped her to perceive who was right in front of her.

The promises of God can be right in front of you, yet you are so focused on the problem, that you do not even see the promises. She said I perceive that thou art a prophet, and her perception had a direct impact on her future actions. She came for water but she left the pail at the well and went back to town telling everyone who would listen about the prophet. Everyone knew her life was a mess, but the way she came back from the well inspired people to go see Jesus. She changed their perception of her and their actions were altered as a result. Perception has a direct impact on your future actions.

The word of the Lord came unto Jeremiah asking what he saw because what Jeremiah perceived would have an impact on his future actions and determine his next steps.

Jeremiah 1:11-12: *11Moreover the word of the Lord came unto me saying, Jeremiah, what seest thou? And I said, I see a rod of an almond tree. 12Then said the Lord unto me, Thou hast well seen: for I will hasten my word to perform it.*

Since Jeremiah was seeing right, the Lord said He would hasten to perform His Word in his life, and He will do the same in our lives. For example, when you are driving your car on the highway at 60 mph and it starts raining cats and dogs, if you are a good driver, you will slow down. Why? Because your vision is not as clear as it was before the rain. When it begins to clear up, you can resume your speed. As it is in the natural, it is in the spirit. When you are seeing right, your life will accelerate. The Lord asked Jeremiah what he saw, knowing that if he could see right, He could hasten to perform His word in Jeremiah's life.

At times, our ability to see right diminishes when we experience painful life circumstances. We can't always choose what happens to us; we can only control what happens inside of us. Don't allow circumstances to alter the perception that God has put in you. When you need to make a decision on anything, seek God for His will and commit to seeing the decision through. Oftentimes, we think that a storm in our lives indicates that we have made a wrong decision. Most of the time, it is just part of the process. God will never change his mind in the middle of a storm and neither should we. He will not speak to you in the middle of a storm and tell you to do something different than what He told you before the storm. Circumstances should never dictate the will of God for our lives, only His Word, spoken or written, should. When a storm comes, commit to seeing right, like Ruth did.

Ruth 1:16: *16 Ruth said, Intreat me not to leave thee, or to return from following after thee: for whither thou goest, I will go; and where thou lodgest, I will lodge: thy people shall be my people, and thy God, my God: 17Where thou diest, will I die, and there will I be buried: the Lord do so to me, and more also, if ought but death part thee and me.*

Naomi had two daughters-in-law, Ruth and Orpah. Naomi means, 'my delight and favor.' Orpah means, 'stiff neck or gazelle.' (Gazelles are nosy, unfocused animals that are always looking around). Eventually Naomi, Ruth and Orpah all were widowed after their husbands died. Naomi informed Ruth and Orpah that she was returning to her country and suggested that they do the same. She continued by advising them to find a nice man and remarry. Ruth and her sister Orpah had different perceptions of their mother-in-law. I can see Orpah attempting to help Ruth understand why they should leave Naomi and go back home. Orpah told Ruth there was nothing that Naomi could do for them. Some people are the same way. They will use you, your gift, and your anointing until you don't have anything else to put in their hand. Then they are ready to go somewhere else. Orpah left and went about her business. Ruth, on the other hand, stayed with Naomi; she had a different perception of her mother-in-law.

Ruth perceived that God connected her to Naomi for a greater purpose than being her mother-in-law. She believed they were to be connected until death parted them. Ruth told Naomi, 'There's something about you, there's something on your life and I know that if I serve you, God will take care of me.' God connected Ruth to Naomi, and she would not let anyone or anything change her perception of that relationship. When we find our holy connection, our holy hook-up, we cannot allow anything to interfere with that relationship.

Ruth's perception of Naomi was a catalyst for her connection to Boaz, the rich landowner who ultimately became her husband. Ruth worked in the field where Boaz saw her, inquired about her and instructed his workers to make sure they dropped some grain for her to glean from the crops. When you stay connected to your holy hook-up, God will purposely drop blessings into your life. (Naomi got a grandson, Ruth got her Boaz, and Orpah probably ended up with a Bozo since she wasn't seeing right.) This is not something I'm saying because I read it in a book; this is what I know because this is how I have lived my life.

Several years ago, after preaching in Atlanta, I received a call from a man who said that as he was preaching in South Carolina that morning, God told him to give me some money. Of course, I agreed. I told him that sounded just like God! In order to get me the money immediately, he asked for my bank account information. True to his word, he made a very large deposit. When I called to thank him, I also gave him permission to keep the account information, so if God spoke to him again, he could deposit it directly. My point is that I was in one place, he was in another place, and still God put me on someone's mind so they could be a blessing to me... all because I see right.

Another time, as I was sitting in my car, someone handed me a card from a guy in California, even though it wasn't my birthday. When I opened it, hundred dollar bills started dropping into my lap – 10 of them! $1,000 cash. The card inside read, "I have been watching how you serve your pastor and the spirit of God spoke to me and told me to sow this into your life. I'm believing for some leaders in my church to see me like you see your pastor." I didn't ask nor was I looking for that. I don't serve to get a response from anyone else. I do it because I love God and the people that I'm serving. You have to be able to see right.

A key to seeing right is learning to hear and respond to the voice of God. John 10:27 says, 27My sheep hear my voice, and I know them, and they follow me.

Doing so gives us what we need to see right. The ability to see right comes from hearing right. Words paint pictures on the canvas of your imagination. When somebody speaks to you, in your mind, you see the image of what they said, not the word. If I say dog, you do not see d-o-g. You see an actual dog. If I say a black dog with a white spot on it, on the canvas of your imagination, you see that kind of dog. Words paint pictures. Because good eyes come from good ears, how you hear and what you hear will determine where you live and how you live. We must determine who we have in our lives that can speak and cause change to come. You will never live beyond what you know, or experience substantial increase, without properly perceiving the person God has placed in your life. They will assist you and speed up your progress.

Look at the people closest to you, the ones you hear from most often. If you listen to them, you will produce as they do. If they are lazy, you will be lazy. If they are trifling, you will be trifling. If they operate in a spirit of excellence, you will too. Regardless of the area of your life that we discuss, you will become like the people you are around most. Strive to be around people who love God, are moving forward and have a positive, teamwork attitude. Our pastor says, 'hang around people who have your answers and avoid those who have your problems.' Even if you must work with negative people, minimize your time with them or you will begin to see their attributes in your life. Think of the last time you were around someone who cussed.

Most likely, you surprised yourself when you said a bad word or two. What you see, how you see it, and whose eyes you see it through are very, very important to your fulfilling purpose in your life. Seeing right will cause you to submit right.

A KEY TO REMEMBER

Perception is Everything!

How you perceive a person determines what you will receive from that person

QUESTIONS FOR PERSONAL GROWTH

How do you see your pastor? Your spouse? Your boss? _____

_____

_____

_____

_____

_____

_____

What standard are you using to see them right?

_____

_____

_____

_____

_____

What are some of the challenges you face when it comes to seeing them right? _____

_____

_____

_____

_____

_____

What will you do to continue or begin seeing them right? _____

_____

_____

_____

_____

_____

_____

NOTES

_____

_____

_____

_____

_____

_____

_____

_____

_____

_____

_____

_____

CHAPTER 2 - SUBMIT RIGHT

In many instances, we hear the word 'submission' and negative feelings immediately begin to surface. These feelings are an indication that we are not seeing right. Webster's Dictionary defines submit as "to give over or yield to the power or authority of another; it is a voluntary attitude of cooperating and assuming responsibility." The prefix "sub" means under and "mission" is an assignment. Therefore, to submit is to get under the assignment or vision of another and play your part in seeing it to completion. Real power exists in submission. To those who don't see right, it appears that those who submit are shrinking, when in actuality they are growing and expressing their confidence and power. Submission is a key to unity, harmony, and winning relationships. It does not mean that we lose our identity; we improve our identity. In the kingdom of God, the way up is down. Most people don't understand this and think they have to be haughty to make themselves bigger and louder to have more power; when in reality, the opposite is true.

Submission always puts you in position to receive favor and to release grace. Whenever you see somebody submit right, they are putting themselves in a better position than the one they are submitting to. For example, Elisha did twice as many miracles as Elijah. When Elijah asked Elisha, "What do you want from me?" He said, "I want a double portion of your spirit." Elijah said, "you ask me a hard thing. I tell you, if you see me when I am taken away, you get it. If you don't see me, you won't" (2 Kings 2:9-10). What's the lesson here? If you don't see right, you won't submit. James 4:7: *7Submit yourselves therefore to God. Resist the devil, and he will flee from you.*

In our own power, we cannot simply resist the devil. We must have the power that flows as a result of true submission to God to have victory over the enemy. That submission becomes evident when you know who God is, what He has put in you to do, and you see Him right. For example, the purpose of a pitcher is to hold water to serve people. If I had two pitchers, one full of water and the other empty, and held them at the same level, the empty pitcher would remain empty. For the empty pitcher to be filled and experience the fullness of its purpose, it must submit to the full pitcher. The full pitcher must also submit in order to fill the empty one. To grow in the kingdom of God, you must submit so you can be poured into, and then you must submit that which is poured into you to others. If you don't submit, you will never fulfill purpose in your life. Remember, real power flows through and by true submission.

Matthew 23:12: *12And whosoever shall exalt himself shall be abased; and he that shall humble himself shall be exalted.*

You have to submit right, with an attitude of humility in order to be exalted. When John the Baptist saw Jesus coming, he said, "Behold the lamb of God which taketh away the sins of the world" (John 1:36). With his natural eyes, John could see the man. In the spirit, he saw something others could not. He perceived that Jesus was the Lamb of God and immediately submitted saying, "I must decrease so He can increase" (John 3:30). The devil doesn't want you to see right or submit right; knowing that when you do, power will flow in and through your life. His plan is to get you unfocused and out of the place of submission and cause you to have a problem seeing your pastor (and others) blessed. When people around you are being blessed, don't start comparing yourself to them and wondering when it will be your turn. Celebrate the blessings of others knowing, that if your neighbors are being blessed, then God is in your neighborhood; and He knows your name, where you live, and your desires. Stay submitted. You are not far behind - and He will give you the desires of your heart!

John the Baptist was preaching, "behold the lamb of God which taketh away the sin of the world." He also said, "I must decrease so he can increase." John had great authority in the earth realm, even having his own disciples. John would go out into the wilderness, start preaching, and people would come from miles around to hear him because of his authority. Yet when Jesus entered the picture, he submitted to His authority and, as a result, the power of God flowed in and through his life.

But there was a place where John the Baptist started seeing wrong. He attended an event with the king, saw some things happening there and started talking about them. The king heard what John said, got mad and had him thrown in jail. While in jail, he realized that Jesus, his cousin, hadn't come to see him. John was focused on the wrong thing and as a result, he stopped submitting right. John asked his disciples, 'Does Jesus know I'm in jail and hasn't come to see about me?' The disciples said, 'Exactly.' They continued by telling John that Jesus was out laying hands on people and healing the sick, rather than coming to see about him.

Then John the Baptist started talking about the ministry and Jesus. 'If it wasn't for me, his ministry wouldn't be all that. I'm the one who is running the ministry of helps around here, putting everything together. I'm the one who said, behold the lamb of God that will take away the sins of the world and I must decrease so he can increase. It was my influence that even got the ministry to where it is and got Jesus to where He is today!' (Of course, I'm paraphrasing.) Can you imagine how John felt? Have you ever served someone and felt like they weren't there when you needed them? I hope you are seeing that this is how people will respond toward their pastor and/or leadership when they stop submitting right. After all that attitude and talking with the disciples, John decided to send Jesus a message. 'Go find Jesus and ask Him, are you the one or should we look for another?'

John was offended because he was in trouble and Jesus didn't make John's urgency his emergency.

We do the same thing. We get offended with our leaders and it causes us to move from the place of submission. We get offended - "off-ended" - OFF of the Word and we END the process of the Word in our lives. We get offended because we focus on the person in front of us rather than the anointing of God on their lives. We get caught up in those cliques, hanging around our friends, allowing them to poison our minds and attitudes, and before you know it, we are not submitting the way we should.

John sends his disciples, his clique, to ask Jesus his question. When they find Him, He's preaching and teaching. They interrupt Him to ask, "John the Baptist wants to know, are you the one or should 'we' look for another?" Who is 'we?' How did 'we' get involved in John's offense? John is the one locked up in jail and offended, so how did it become 'we?' "We" got involved because John was offended and poured bitterness into his disciples. Jesus responded saying, "you go back and you tell John, the blind see, the lame walk, the deaf hear, and blessed are those who are not offended in me." He sent John a message saying blessed or empowered to prosper are they that are not offended in me.

His message to John was to stay in a place of submission; because that is where the power flows. Not only did Jesus teach it with His words, He lived it in His actions.

When John's disciples left, Jesus turned to His disciples that were standing behind him. They were angry and waiting for Jesus to give them the word to go deal with John, especially Peter. I can imagine Peter now, he was probably shaking his head, saying, 'Lord, all you have to do is give me the word and I will go down in that prison and cut that boy's head off. I missed the first guy, but I won't miss this one' (John 18:10). *(In the Garden of Gethsemane when Peter cut off the guard's ear, he couldn't have been aiming for his ear; Who does that? When you swing a sword at somebody's head, you are trying to chop off his whole head, not just his ear. If you ask me, that guard just moved.)* Jesus could have signed John's death certificate with the wrong words. Instead, Jesus said, "there is not a man born of a woman greater than John the Baptist" (Luke 7:28). Jesus knew that getting out of the place of submission would cause a power failure.

Even though John was obviously wrong, Jesus loved him enough to cover his sin. Just like in Acts 16:26 when Paul and Silas prayed, God caused an earthquake to shake the jail hard enough for the doors to open and Peter went free. He could have done the same thing for John had he remained submissive and prayed instead of complaining. Jesus saw right so he could continue to submit right and ultimately serve right by teaching John and the disciples that real power comes through and by submission. Let's look at another example of someone who submitted right.

Matthew 8:7-9: *⁷And Jesus saith unto him, I will come and heal him. ⁸ The centurion answered and said, Lord, I am not worthy that thou shouldest come under my roof: but speak the word only, and my servant shall be healed. ⁹ For I am a man under authority, having soldiers under me: and I say to this man, Go, and he goeth; and to another, Come, and he cometh; and to my servant, Do this, and he doeth it.*

This centurion went to Jesus to ask him to heal his servant that was at home sick. Jesus agreed. The centurion answered saying that it wasn't necessary for

Jesus to come, all Jesus needed to do was speak and his servant would be healed. When Jesus heard the centurion, He marveled and said unto them that followed Him, "Verily, verily I say unto you I have not found so great faith no not in Israel." In order for you to be in authority, you must first be under authority. As I stated earlier, real power comes through and by submission. The centurion demonstrated that he understood—and had faith—in Jesus' authority. He was actually saying to Jesus, 'I've been watching you and I can tell that like me, you are a man under authority. So, speak the word from right where you are and just like my servants obey me, sickness will obey you and my servant will be healed.

Luke 7:37-38: *36 And one of the Pharisees desired him that he would eat with him. And he went into the Pharisee's house, and sat down to meat. 37 And, behold, a woman in the city, which was a sinner, when she knew that Jesus sat and ate in the Pharisee's house, brought an alabaster box of ointment, 38 And stood at his feet behind him weeping, and began to wash his feet with tears, and did wipe them with the hairs of her head, and kissed his feet, and anointed them with the ointment.*

Jesus was having a meal at the house of one of the Pharisees and people were bringing money and gifts to Him. During this meeting, a woman came with an alabaster box filled with a very precious and expensive ointment.

When I studied this story, it was intriguing to learn that Jesus had previously cast devils out of this woman, a prostitute. In that day, prostitutes would use good, costly perfume to seduce a man into paying for her services. This was how she made money and the ointment was very important and valuable to her. She broke the alabaster box, poured the ointment on Jesus' head and started rubbing His feet with her hair. His disciples, especially Judas, saw this and got irritated saying, 'What a waste! He could have sold that perfume, gotten a year's worth of pay and put the money in the treasury. We could have kept some of the money and gave some to the poor. He is just sitting there letting her waste that perfume that's worth so much money.' Judas got everybody thinking about how it would have helped the poor had the perfume been sold rather than the prostitute wasting it by rubbing it on Jesus' feet. None of them were really thinking about the poor—including Judas. The irony was that these were not Jesus' enemies, these were men 'submitted' to and walking with Jesus. We know this since Jesus would send them out to cast out devils in His name. They stopped seeing right, which made them stop submitting right.

Judas left that meeting fired up; he was upset and more than likely saying within himself, 'I need to look out for me now; I've got to make sure I am taken care of.' You can tell that Judas was thinking like this because when he got to the chief priests and elders, he asked them what they would give him to turn Jesus over to them. They simply offered Judas some silver and the deal was made to betray Jesus (Matthew 26:15).

As Judas returns to the meeting, Jesus—operating in the Spirit—says, "one of you will betray me." The disciples knew that they were just complaining about the prostitute breaking the alabaster box and rubbing it on Jesus' feet. As they begin to think about what happened, the Bible says they were exceedingly sorrowful and started saying, "Lord, is it I?" Every single one of them said the same thing, "Lord, is it I?" The word lord means master, ruler, and controller. What they were actually saying was 'Lord, I had a bad thought and even said some bad things about you when the prostitute broke that alabaster box. It may not be me, but if it is, just tell me. I don't want to be out of the place of submission with you. I am willing to change.' All of them referred to Jesus as 'Lord,' except for Judas who said, "Master, is it I?" The word master means teacher. Judas at one point called Jesus Lord, but when he got offended he called him "Master" (teacher). (Matthew 26:25)

In previous times when Judas looked at Jesus as "Lord," it meant that he would do as Jesus said. As "Master" (teacher), Judas was basically refusing to submit. The other disciples were saying, 'I'm submitting to you; what you say to me I will do, and I will obey because I am giving you that authority in my life.' Judas, on the other hand, was saying, 'I like some of the things you say. But I won't do everything you say because I am no longer submitting myself to you.' Let me pause right here to say this... never, ever despise seeing anyone being blessed, especially your pastor and other leaders. Look at what happened to Judas.

The guilt became too much for him and he became so distraught that he went out and hung himself. When you are out of the place of submission, the devil will seize the opportunity to steal from you, kill you, and otherwise destroy you.

Even in a relationship, submission is vital. When a man and woman decide to marry, they do so from the same level. Once they say, 'I do,' the female must retire and submit. As I said earlier, she doesn't lose her identity, she improves it. When you put your spouse's needs above your own, in true submission, only then will the marital relationship thrive. When you get a couple operating like that, you will see real power flowing in and through their relationship and consequently their lives. The same is true in our relationships with our parents. When you honor your father and mother as the Bible commands, your days will be long and it will be well with you (Ephesians 6:2). Submission is the key to longevity in our lives and our relationships.

1 Peter 5:6: *6 Humble yourselves therefore under the mighty hand of God, that he may exalt you in due time.*

Understand that in the kingdom of God, the way up is down, unlike in the world where the way up is to step on others. Anytime God tells you to submit or retire from a position, He has something greater for you. Some people think, when I submit, nobody will be able to find me. However, David was in the field, taking care of his father's sheep and God found him. His own father forgot about him, but God did not and He hasn't forgotten about you either.

There are two kinds of submission. Basically, there is a worldly way and there is a godly way to submit.

GODLY SUBMISSION	WORLDLY SUBMISSION
Birthed from the inside, out of love in the heart, you humble yourself	Imposed from the outside; the world and its laws will make you submit because the system humbles you
Motivated by agape love that wants to give to the object of its affection	Motivated by self-interest
Emphasizes interdependence on one another	Emphasizes independence and self

Looks for ways to serve others	Looks for others to serve them
Causes you to look for ways to create an advantage for someone else	Causes you to put your needs and interests above others
Causes you to submit authentically, knowing that God always looks at your heart	Causes you to pretend to submit

If we do not learn to submit in a godly manner, we can never hope to fulfill destiny and purpose in life because the way up is down. Many people will pretend to submit to further their personal agenda. Some pretend to submit to traffic laws by speeding down the highway with a radar detector in their car. That is not real submission. They are only attempting to avoid the pain by not getting a speeding ticket. If you are only submitting when you think people are watching, you've forgotten that we serve a God who sees everything.

Some business owners pretend to submit to get more business. Some church members only submit when the pastor or other leaders are watching. Our pastor has asked us to be on time for church services. To be submissive would mean that we show up—on time—consistently. Instead, some people show up late, thinking that they're fooling everyone else when God sees they are not submitting to the rules of the house. We can be on time to work or a sporting event, but can't be on time for our assignment in church? Then we cry out, 'bless me Lord Jesus, hurry up' and we aren't on time ourselves. How is it that we have forgotten that God knows all and sees all? He's the only one who matters, and we're not fooling Him.

Even Jesus submitted His will to His father. Jesus healed the sick, without concern for Himself. There is not one time in the Bible where Jesus healed himself. Actually, when His cousin died, Jesus went up into the mountain to pray and deal with his death. The Bible says that while he was there, a multitude of folks came to him with all kinds of sicknesses and problems, asking Him to pray for them. Jesus set aside all of his issues and started praying and healing people; an example of true submission. Jesus not only lived this, he taught about the importance of seeing right and submitting right.

John 13:16: *16 Verily, verily, I say unto you, The servant is not greater than his lord; neither he that is sent greater than he that sent him.*

Jesus said that although He was sent by God, He still was not greater than God. He submitted Himself to the will of God saying, "I only do what I see my Father do, only say what I hear my Father say. When you see me, you see Him" (John 5:19). What do people say about you? You say you are a member of such-and-such ministry and you're connected with your pastor and church leaders; can anyone see that in you? Will your leaders confirm that you are submissive?

Philippians 2:6-9: *6 Who, being in the form of God, thought it not robbery to be equal with God: 7 But made himself of no reputation, and took upon him the form of a servant, and was made in the likeness of men: 8 And being found in fashion as a man, he humbled himself, and became obedient unto death, even the death of the cross. 9 Wherefore God also hath highly exalted him, and given him a name which is above every name.*

Jesus was obedient to the death. He humbled himself and God highly exalted Him; therefore, when you humble yourself, you will be exalted. My pastor (Michael Freeman) is also my younger brother. Because I see him right, it has caused me to submit right. Submitting right has caused me to serve right and people all across the country talk about how I serve my brother. However, I am not submitted to my brother, I am submitted to my pastor. Our spiritual relationship weighs much more than our natural relationship; he is more my pastor than my brother.

Matthew 10:39: [39] *He that findeth his life shall lose it; and he that loseth his life for my sake shall find it.*

Some church leaders who have never heard me preach or teach call for me to come to their churches to minister as a result of this revelation. One such pastor was so impressed that he asked me to come to his church to share with his leaders for two days. After ministering, I asked him why he invited me to his church. He stated that he saw how I was submissive to my pastor and anybody who would submit like that had to have something to say. He said: this is the kind of person that I would want to come and talk to the people of my church.

Because I set aside my personal agenda for God's agenda, I ended up fulfilling my personal agenda. God has opened many doors for me to do what I love doing—serving pastors and leaders in making God's people better. Luke 16:12 states, 12And if ye have not been faithful in that which is another man's, who shall give you that which is your own. Remember when we learn to see right and submit right, then God can depend on us to serve right!

A KEY TO REMEMBER

The Way Up is Down

Submission does not mean that you lose your identity, you will improve your identity.

QUESTIONS FOR PERSONAL GROWTH

On a scale of 1-10, rate your level of submission to

your pastor? Your spouse? Your boss? _____

_____

_____

_____

_____

_____

_____

Is it easy or hard to submit to each of them? Why?

_____

_____

_____

_____

What are some of the challenges you face when it comes to submitting to each of them? _____

_____

_____

_____

_____

_____

If you have a problem submitting (i.e., taking instruction) to them, why? How will you correct it?

_____

_____

_____

_____

_____

NOTES

_____

_____

_____

_____

_____

_____

_____

_____

_____

_____

_____

_____

_____

_____

CHAPTER 3 - SERVE RIGHT

Although there are many definitions of serve, for our intent and purpose, to serve means: to work for another, to render assistance, to act as a servant, to be worthy of reliance or trust, to help, to furnish or supply with something needed or desired, to answer the need of another. In churches, we use 'Minister' as a title. By definition, minister means to run errands for, a waiter, to assist, to benefit someone else, to serve. Therefore, true ministry (serving) is an act of worship unto God.

Often we get caught up not wanting to serve because we forget that when we minister or serve people, we are also serving God. You cannot serve God without serving people. Serving is the way to fulfillment in this life. People who don't serve often are nasty, unhappy, bitter people while servants are warm, friendly, caring, happy people with the heart of God. Matthew 25:37-40 in the Message Bible reads: "Then those 'sheep' are going to say, 'Master, what are you talking about? When did we ever see you hungry and feed you, thirsty and give you a drink? And when did we ever see you sick or in prison and come to you?' Then the King will say, 'I'm telling the solemn truth:

Whenever you did one of these things to someone overlooked or ignored, that was me—you did it to me.'

As you can see, God takes our serving personally, whether we are helping or harming others. In Acts 9:4-5, Jesus asked Saul: "4Saul, Saul, why persecutest thou me? 5And he said, Who are thou, Lord? And the Lord said, I am Jesus whom thou persecutest: [it is] hard for thee to kick against the pricks."

Even though Saul never personally did anything to Jesus, when he was causing harm to Christians, Jesus responded as though Saul was doing it to Him. This viewpoint can also be seen in marital relationships. Some time ago, a waiter was being rude to my wife. At the same time, it felt as though he was being rude to me. I was thinking, 'waiter, waiter, why persecutest thou me?' It was clear the waiter didn't understand that my wife and I are one, and that being rude to my wife was the same as being rude to me. If God connects Himself to the people whom we are serving, we must see beyond the people and serve them as though we were serving God. Remember, those who are great in the kingdom of God will be servants to others. Matthew 20:26 states: 26But it shall not be so among you: but whosoever will be great among you, let him be your minister.

It is through our service that we use our God-given gifts to give His people an advantage in life. That is how God defines greatness in His kingdom. As we discussed in Chapter 2, the way up in the kingdom of God is down. Remember, we don't have to step on, connive, use, deceive, or otherwise hurt people to get ahead; simply humble yourself and serve right and God will exalt you. 'But he that is greatest among you shall be your servant' (Matthew 23:11).

When we teach others to serve, we are showing them the pathway to greatness. God designed you to fulfill and meet needs in the lives of others. When you serve right, God will not forget you; all of your needs will be met as well.

Psalms 100:2 gives us guidelines for serving:

2 Serve the LORD with gladness: come before his presence with singing.

We must serve with a spirit of excellence and a heart of gladness in everything that we say and do, realizing that serving the Lord is a privilege. Did you get that? Serving the Lord is a privilege! We should want to serve rather than feel like we have to serve. Who wants to be served by someone who is angry or has a bad attitude? Your attitude will always go before you, as a friend or an enemy. It will take you up or down. The Bible is clear that in order to reap the benefits of serving, we must serve as God ordained.

Job 36:11: *11 If they obey and serve him, they shall spend their days in prosperity, and their years in pleasures.*

Notice, the scripture reads serve and obey. Some serve, but don't obey—trying to do it their own way. We cannot give God what we think He should have and expect Him to bless it. The Bible says, there is a way that seems right to a man but at the end of that way is death (Proverbs 14:12). We must serve out of a heart of obedience that is apparent in our attitude as we flow in our assignment, and use our gift(s) to increase and promote others. What would happen if we became others-minded, asking 'What can I do to make your day?' or 'What can I do to make you better?' or 'How can I use my gift(s) and anointing to cause increase

and give you an advantage?' What if we used our
gift(s) for the benefit of the church or ministry God
placed us in? Our prayers should include asking God to
show us how to use the gift(s) that He placed inside of
us to cause increase and promotion to come to the
vision we are currently part of.

Most often, we serve the world with our gifts
because our jobs and businesses give us money in
exchange. For some, money is the primary motivator
for using their gift(s), rather than being motivated by
furthering the kingdom of God. Recognize that God
gave you those gifts to bless others; being paid is an
extra bonus. If you find yourself talking and thinking
about money often, it is an indication that you don't
truly understand the principles of money.

Do not allow the pursuit of money to consume you
or money will elude you like the butterflies we all
chased as children. Rather, chase opportunities to give
people an advantage in life. You will attract money by
being the person God created you to be. Matthew 6:33
says, 'to seek first the kingdom of God and His
righteousness and all these things that the Gentiles are
seeking will be added unto you.' Money will chase you,
if you serve right. When you get that revelation,

serving becomes the most fulfilling thing in life as you assist others and they assist you. Nothing compares to the joy of blessing others. When you follow the principles and do the things God created you to do, all your needs will be met—even the financial ones.

Most businesses have a customer service policy – guidelines for serving and being served. When the church establishes guidelines for serving, people get offended. You cannot come to church and operate outside the guidelines of the house (translates: 'do what you want to do') and think that God will bless your disobedience. For example, in Numbers 20:8-12, God told Moses to speak to the rock. Instead, Moses did it his way and hit the rock twice. As a result of his disobedience, Moses was not able to lead the Israelites into the Promised Land. The scriptures are clear that we must serve and obey to get the promised results. We must learn to serve right, like the Corinthian Church.

1 Corinthians 16:15-16: *15 I beseech you, brethren, (ye know the house of Stephanas, that it is the first fruits of Achaia, and that they have addicted themselves to the ministry of the saints,) 16 That ye*

submit yourselves unto such, and to everyone that helpeth with us, and laboureth.

The people in the house of Stephanas were addicted to ministry. You couldn't stop them from serving. They had an addiction to serving and so should we. Have you ever been addicted to anything - alcohol, marijuana, cigarettes? Webster's Dictionary defines addiction as "the state of being enslaved to a habit or practice or to something that is psychologically or physically habit-forming, as narcotics." For instance, cigarette addictions often cause you to smoke one, put it out, and then a half-hour later feel as though you need to smoke another. With all of the 'no smoking' laws that have been enacted over the last decade, this addiction must be fed outside the comfort of public buildings and restaurants. Even when it's cold, addicted smokers will forego their personal comfort to respond to the call of that little cigarette. Therefore, we must learn to forego our personal comfort to use our gifts and talents in service to meet the needs of others. In short, we must be addicted to serving like Peter's mother-in-law.

Matthew 8:14-15 explains: *14And when Jesus was come into Peter's house, he saw his wife's mother laid, and sick of a fever. [15]And he touched her hand, and the fever left her: and she arose, and ministered unto them.*

She had an addiction to serving. She was in bed with a fever, not feeling well. Jesus touched her hand and she was healed. The first thing she did was to start serving people and ministering to their needs. She really had a love for people and was fulfilled by serving them. Do you know people like that? My wife is that way, addicted to serving. No matter how she feels or what's going on in our lives, she makes a way to be there for others. That addiction is contagious. She's so serious and committed to serving, that together, we have built our lives on serving others both personally and at our church.

How great a church would we have if we all had a serving addiction? A great church is a serving church. All of the ministry leaders and members would look for ways to ensure that every visitor and member had a positive, life-changing experience at every service. Everyone would be ministered to, greeted warmly, made comfortable, and shown the love of Jesus. Can you image a church like that? Attendance would skyrocket. People come to church looking for their needs to be met. When we serve right, we make people feel special, valuable, and cared for. People don't care how much you know, until they know how much you care. When they find out how much you care, they will be open to listening to how much you know. If you ever hope to flow in greatness, you must learn how to serve. Show me a person who knows how to serve right, and I'll show you a person who loves God.

Hebrews 6:10: *¹⁰ For God is not unrighteous to forget your work and labour of love, which ye have showed toward his name, in that ye have ministered to the saints, and do minister.*

The Message Bible says, "God doesn't miss anything. He knows perfectly well all the love you've shown him by helping needy Christians, and that you keep at it." You demonstrate your love for God by meeting the needs of others. Many of us give lip service saying, 'God I love you.' No, God says show me by serving with an excellent spirit motivated by agape love; with no strings attached. God will use you as a distribution channel to get things through you to His people. Serve so you can be a blessing to someone else and God will move in your situations on your behalf. All you should be concerned about is the other person. *[Put yourself aside, and help others get ahead. Don't be obsessed with getting your own advantage. Forget yourselves long enough to lend a helping hand (Philippians 2:4-6, Message Bible)].* You say you want to be like Jesus, right? Jesus was others-minded. He put others before Himself. When you have others on your mind, God has you on His mind. Even though Jesse forgot about David, God didn't.

In 1 Samuel 16, God told Nathan the prophet to go to Jesse's house and anoint one of his sons. Jesse began to parade his tall, well-dressed boys before the prophet. When the man of God saw Jesse's sons, he said 'not one of these are God's anointed.' God told him, 'don't look at the outward appearance. When the first son passed, he said, 'no.' He said. 'no' to the second, third, fourth, fifth, sixth, and seventh sons. None of them was the one God sent him to anoint. Nathan had to ask Jesse if he had any other sons. Can you believe that? Then Jesse remembered his other son, a shepherd named David. How do you forget you have a son? When I looked at the scripture more carefully, I found that David was born out of wedlock and Jesse put him out in the pasture with a few sheep to hide his indiscretion (which is why when the bear and the lion came, he had to kill them; he was protecting the few that he was watching). The Bible says David was like a stranger to his own brothers and a foreigner to his mother's children. The prophet tells Jesse to send for David. Compared to his big, strong brothers, David was a little guy with red hair. Jesse couldn't imagine that David would be the son that God had chosen, but he was. [70] He chose David also his **servant**, and took him from the sheepfolds (Psalms 78:70). *(Emphasis mine.)*

David was faithful over the little that he was given and even when his own father forgot about him, God didn't. God took David from the sheepfold and brought him into great positions because he knew how to serve right. Anytime you serve God, by serving his people, you will get God's attention. Don't get mad when your labor seems to go unnoticed by man, just keep serving. God said, 'He will not forget your work and labor of love.' He will bless and protect you, even in the face of your enemies. [22] The LORD redeemeth the soul of his servants: and none of them that trust in him shall be desolate (Psalms 34:22).

In this scripture, redeem means 'to rescue, ransom, to preserve, and to deliver by any means.' God said that when you serve right, you will receive His favor. God will redeem His servants, by any means necessary, if you trust Him and serve Him. In Daniel 3, Shadrach, Meshach, and Abed-nego were good friends with the king. Most of the king's subjects didn't like them and looked for a way to get rid of them. The people appealed to the king to create a golden image for everyone to bow and pray to when he played certain music. Anyone who didn't do as he commanded would be cast into a fiery furnace. The king agreed. When the music played, Shadrach, Meshach, and Abed-nego wouldn't bow and the people reported it to the king, reminding him of what he said; even painting a vision of his entire kingdom ignoring his future commands when they heard that the three boys didn't bow. The king called for the three Hebrew boys who confirmed that they would not bow to the golden image. Because the king liked them, he said, "I will give you one more chance. If you don't bow this time, I'm going to throw you into the furnace." Consider this passage of scripture found in Daniel 3:16-19:

¹⁶ Shadrach, Meshach, and Abed-nego, answered and said to the king, O Nebuchadnezzar, we are not careful to answer thee in this matter. *¹⁷ If it be so*, our God whom we serve is able to deliver us from the burning fiery furnace, and he will deliver us out of thine hand, O king. ¹⁸ ***But if not,*** be it known unto thee, O king, that we will not serve thy gods, nor worship the golden image which thou hast set up. ¹⁹ Then was Nebuchadnezzar full of fury, and the form of his visage was changed against Shadrach, Meshach, and Abed-nego: therefore he spake, and commanded that they should heat the furnace one seven times more than it was wont to be heated. *(Emphasis mine.)*

Shadrach and the others told the king, if it be so, if you do what you said, we don't have to think about this… our God, whom we serve, is able and will deliver us out of your hands. He will deliver us out of the fiery furnace. But if not, doesn't mean that there is a possibility that God won't deliver them, even though a lot of ministers preach that. What they were saying is that if the king didn't send them to the furnace and allowed them to go, they still would not bow nor serve the king's god. They said, 'the God whom we serve' will deliver us. They were professing their commitment to serve only their God. Can you say that 'the God whom I serve will deliver me?' Remember, he redeems His servants by any means necessary.

Of course, this angered the king even more and he commanded the guards to make the furnace seven times hotter than normal, and throw the three Hebrew boys into the fire. When they did as they were instructed, the guards were totally burned up. If you are throwing someone into a furnace, you do not throw them in with you being in front of them, you get behind them. If they were in front, I see how the guards got burned up. Think about this: How did the guards get burned up from behind the boys, outside the furnace? The fire had to go around Shadrach, Meshach, and Abed-nego to get to the guards. This happened outside the furnace. Most people focus on God's protection in the furnace, not realizing that the protection started before they were even thrown into the fire. He did this for His servants. God honored their faith and protected them, by any means necessary—just as He promised. Do what God called you to do, with all your might; give your very best and God will always take care of you. He did it for the three Hebrew boys, He did it for Paul, and He will do it for you.

Acts 27:9-11: *9 Now when much time was spent, and when sailing was now dangerous, because the fast was now already past, Paul admonished them, 10 And said unto them, Sirs, I perceive that this voyage will be with hurt and much damage, not only of the lading and ship, but also of our lives. 11 Nevertheless the centurion believed the master and the owner of the ship, more than those things which were spoken by Paul.*

The Apostle Paul was a prisoner on a ship. He told his captors that should they continue the voyage, there would be considerable danger and potential damage. Of course, they listened to the owner of the ship rather than the prisoner. A terrible storm ensued that threatened their very lives. All of a sudden, Paul stood up and said, "for there stood by me this night an angel of God, whose I am and whom I serve." He was telling them that the God he served was not going to allow any harm to come to them.

How many can say, 'God I serve you and because I serve you, I can always count on you to serve me.' God will always honor you. Don't get upset when you don't get recognized or people don't pat you on the back. Don't be concerned about whether or not people call your name or even remember your name in association with all the work you do. Definitely don't stop serving because you haven't been acknowledged. The only person you should care about calling/knowing your name is Almighty God and hearing Him say, 'this is my beloved son or daughter, in whom I'm well pleased.'

Galatians 6:9 tells us, *⁹And let us not be weary in well doing: for in due season we shall reap, if we faint not.*

As long as you don't allow yourself to get weary and continue to serve, no one can stop you from being blessed. Serve from the heart, from the inside-out, so that what others do or don't do won't stop you. Often we see others sitting around doing nothing and we get upset because it seems like we're doing all the work. Don't ever get tired of serving.

Most of the married couples that come into my office are weary because they aren't serving each other right. Marriage is all about serving and meeting the needs of your spouse, and when their needs are not met, problems will arise. Conversely, when you serve right and meet their needs, the problems will go away. For example, the wife in a couple I was counseling complained that her need for affection was not being met by her husband. In our discussion, we talked about how her husband could meet her need through serving her, giving her what she needed, rather than what he thought she should have. Once he started to serve her the way she needed to be served, the problem was resolved and their marriage was back on track. To have a great marriage, you cannot be selfish. Great marriages come through and by serving your spouse.

Let me address the singles here for a moment. In my book, "Integrity Below the Belt," we discuss how singles should not focus on kissing, touching and other things. (Details for purchase are on the back page of this book.) What they should focus on is how their prospective mate serves. Observe how they serve their parents; are they respectful and accountable? Do they help to clean up after family gatherings and do other things around the house for them? How do they serve you? Does that person open doors for you, if you're a woman; or if you're man, is she respectful? How do they serve at church or do they? How do they serve their supervisor, do they show up late and leave early? These are not questions to ask, these are actions to observe. If they don't know how to serve in these situations, rest assured they won't know how to serve you in a marital situation.

In Genesis 29, Jacob showed that serving was a lifestyle for him. When he asked Laban to marry Rachel, Laban told him that if he served seven years, he would give her to him. At the end of the time, Jacob was excited to finally marry his bride, only to find out that Laban had lied and deceived him by giving him his older daughter, Leah. When Jacob realized that his bride was not his beloved Rachel, he confronted Laban only to be told that he had to serve another seven years if he wanted to marry Rachel. And he did it. He served Laban a total of 14 years to get the hand of Rachel, and once he did, he still continued to serve her father. Jacob served Laban so well that everything Laban had increased. Is serving a lifestyle for you, like it was Jacob? Are you prepared for a life of service to your spouse like Jacob was? Be sure that serving is a lifestyle, not an event, for both you and the person whom you are marrying. Never serve just to get something out of it; when you do, it becomes work. You will always benefit when you serve others as an expression of your love for people.

Serving is not a fair-weather activity. We have to be prepared to serve no matter how good or bad things are for us. If you say you are a follower of Jesus Christ, you should be serving others.

One of the greatest examples of serving is shown in John 13:1-17: *¹Now before the feast of the passover, when Jesus knew that his hour was come that he should depart out of this world unto the Father, having loved his own which were in the world, he loved them unto the end. ²And supper being ended, the devil having now put into the heart of Judas Iscariot, Simon's son, to betray him; ³Jesus knowing that the Father had given all things into his hands, and that he was come from God, and went to God; ⁴He riseth from supper, and laid aside his garments; and took a towel, and girded himself. ⁵After that he poureth water into a bason, and began to wash the disciples' feet, and to wipe them with the towel wherewith he was girded. ⁶Then cometh he to Simon Peter: and Peter saith unto him, Lord, dost thou wash my feet? 7Jesus answered and said unto him, What I do thou knowest not now; but thou shalt know hereafter. 8Peter saith unto him, Thou shalt never wash my feet. Jesus answered him, If I wash thee not, thou hast no part with me. 9Simon Peter saith unto him, Lord, not my feet only, but also my hands and my head. 10Jesus saith to him, He that is washed needeth not save to wash his feet, but is clean every whit: and ye are clean, but not all. 11For he knew who should betray him; therefore said he, Ye are not all clean. 12So after he had washed their feet, and had taken his garments, and was set down again, he said unto them, Know ye what I have done to you? 13Ye call me Master and Lord: and ye say well; for so I am. 14If I then, your Lord and Master, have washed your feet; ye also ought to wash one another's feet. 15For I have given you an example, that ye should do as I have done to you. 16Verily, verily, I say unto you, The servant is not greater than his lord; neither he that is sent greater than he that sent him. 17If ye know these things, happy are ye if ye do them.*

There are two principles that are abundantly clear here. First, no matter how bad things are going for us, we have no excuse for not serving others. Jesus knew He was about to die, but because He loved the disciples unto the end, that love motivated Him to serve—when in the natural, you would think He would want to be served. Rather than that, His love for them kept Him off of His own mind.

In verse 4, Jesus laid aside His garment and girded himself with a towel so that he could wash the feet of the disciples. He knew that the garment could possibly get in the way of Him serving. That is akin to laying aside His title and His deity to serve them. Part of the reason we have so much trouble serving others is that we don't want to lay aside our titles and positions to do so. Even Peter got upset when Jesus started washing feet. In his mind, this was too small a task for Jesus the Christ to do. Peter did not understand that if you are too big to do a small job, you are too small to do a big job.

After washing their feet, Jesus put His garment back on and began to share that serving was the way to fulfillment. Verses 15-17, 'for I've given you an example and you will be happy if you do these things.' [paraphrased]

Second, the presence of evil did not hinder Him from serving. Of course, Jesus knew that Judas was going to betray Him, but He didn't focus on His own troubles, He focused on the people who needed Him in that moment. Can you imagine washing the disciples' feet and getting to Judas knowing that he had just betrayed you? Would you have washed his feet or would you have poured the water over his head? Regardless of what you're going through, don't allow the actions of others to hinder your serving. No matter where you serve, serve in such a way that when people leave your presence they stand a little taller, smile a bit longer, and say to themselves... there's something different about you.

When you see right, you will submit right. When you submit right, you will serve right. When you serve right, you do it from the heart. Matthew 6:21 says your heart is an indication of what you value and where your treasure is. Serving right will cause you to sow right.

A KEY TO REMEMBER

Serving is the way to fulfillment in life.

It is through our service that we use our God-given gifts to give others the advantage in life.

QUESTIONS FOR PERSONAL GROWTH

On a scale of 1-10, how would you rate your level of service to your pastor, your spouse and your boss?

_____

_____

_____

_____

_____

_____

How is your attitude while serving them? Why?

_____

_____

_____

_____

Do you allow others or circumstances to stop you

from serving? If so, why? _____

_____

_____

_____

_____

_____

What will you do to improve your service to them?

_____

_____

_____

_____

_____

_____

NOTES

CHAPTER 4 - SOW RIGHT

The spirit of God spoke to me saying, "I am not as concerned about your living, as I am about your giving." With that revelation, my wife and I declared that we would give more that year than we had in any other. We found that locked in your giving is your living, not the other way around. When you focus on others, God will increase your giving to others and your living for yourself.

Proverbs 11:25: *25The generous soul will be made rich, And he who waters will also be watered himself (NKJV).*

The Message Bible says, 'The one who blesses others is abundantly blessed; those who help others are helped.' Your ability to give more is an indication that you have more and are living better. Some people focus on providing their own living, thinking they can't afford to give. It is time for us to move past that limited thinking and realize that until we learn to give and to focus on the needs of others, we won't ever live the life that we desire. As you open your hand to be a blessing to others, God will fill that same hand with blessings for you. This is God's way to increase you. The law of sowing and reaping, found in Luke 6:38 states, "Give and it shall come back to you, good measure, pressed down, shaken together shall men give into your bosom. For with the same measure that ye mete withal it shall be measured to you again."

Webster's defines the word "sow" as "to plant, to set in motion, to begin an enterprise." That got me thinking, when a person gives or sows, he or she sets things in motion. On the other hand, if you don't sow, you won't set anything in motion. God wants us to activate His plan to increase us.

In order to sow right, we must do so with the right attitude. We are to give out of obedience to the scriptures, since we were created to give. Also, we should be motivated by the same agape love that moved God to sacrifice and give His only Son. He demonstrated His love to us and we should demonstrate our love back to Him and others by obeying His Word in our giving.

Most Christians have missed the mark by making Luke 6:38 the motive for giving, rather than the reward of giving. We have also missed the mark by not realizing that there are two kingdoms in operation. There is the kingdom of God, which is represented by light, and the kingdom of Satan that is represented by darkness. A king is known for how well he takes care of the people in his kingdom. The ruler that runs the system in the kingdom of darkness doesn't care anything about his people. In that system you have to fend for yourself. When you receive Jesus Christ as Lord and Savior of your life, He delivers you from darkness and into the marvelous light. If you're not careful, you will take the mindset from the kingdom of darkness along with you. In the kingdom of light, the King takes care of all his citizens and their needs based on the principles of reaping and sowing.

In the kingdom of God, these principles apply: (1) you always reap what you sow. Whatever you put in is what you are going to get out. If you sow an apple seed, you are going to get an apple tree, not an orange tree. (2) You always reap more than you sow. If you sow an apple seed, you'll reap more than one apple. You are going to get many apples; for many seasons to come, good measure, pressed down, shaken together, and running over.

Please note, the devil will attempt to stop you from

giving, although he will never attempt to stop you from spending. He knows that when you give, God's plan for increase is set in motion; when you spend, the money is gone. The enemy's plan is not just to stop you from giving, but if you give, he wants you to give grudgingly and out of necessity, rather than cheerfully. That's not God's plan for increase.

2 Corinthians 9:7: *7Every man according as he purposeth in his heart, so let him give; not grudgingly, or of necessity: for God loveth a cheerful giver.*

Being a cheerful giver shows that you are fully participating in God's plan for increase; it is an indication that you know how to sow right. Often you will hear the un-cheerful and the un-churched complain that churches talk too much about money. Statistically speaking, the average person thinks about money more than 30 percent of the day. We think about how to get it, how to keep it, how to save it, and how to spend it.

Additionally, most Americans spend 40-plus hours a week at a job—more time than they spend with their families—in pursuit of money. It amazes me that we don't think we should talk more about money, especially considering we spend most of our waking hours pursuing and thinking about it.

God gave to us cheerfully, realizing there was no way that we could ever pay him back. John 3:16 is our model for giving: [16]For God so loved the world, that He gave his only begotten son, that whosoever believeth in him should not perish, but have everlasting life.

Let's look at what motivated God to give. He loved us, so He gave. If we love Him, we will give. There is no discussion in this verse about what God gets from His sowing. What He gave however, was an advantage in life to anyone who would accept His gift, and He rescued us out of our perishing predicaments. We must follow His example in our giving and not give with the motive to get; agape love must be our motivation.

Unfortunately, the church has misused Luke 6:38, making the reward for giving their motive for giving. God gives with no strings attached and so should we. When we give with the right motive, then we can release our faith to receive the corresponding, Bible-promised return on our giving. There is a song whose lyrics say;

"I don't know why Jesus loves me,
I don't know why He cares,
I don't know why He sacrificed His life,
Oh, but I'm glad, so glad He did."

We should love and give that way – motivated by agape love, which does not have a reason for its giving.

When we give in the kingdom of God, motivated by love, we satisfy the One we can't see, thereby pushing His buttons, which positions us to receive the expected promise. For example, if you wanted a honeybun from a vending machine, what would you do? You'd count out the money you need, put it into the machine to satisfy the owner whom you don't know and can't see. You would then press D-9, and the arm of the vending machine would begin to move. Then you would position yourself by stooping down to retrieve the honeybun because you know that you have met the requirements of the machine.

Similarly, giving is like the vending machine in that your product/promise was in the unseen arena. You can't touch it—just like the clear window that separated you from the honeybun. When you meet the requirements of the One you can't see, which is God, you can release your faith, just like when you pressed D-9 on the vending machine. The arm in the Spirit starts moving because you have positioned yourself to receive your promise.

In the world's system, in order to reap, you must first sow. In the kingdom you receive first, then you sow. Being that we are in this world but not of this world, we must see beyond the natural. The Bible says, that He gives seed to the sower (2 Corinthians 9:10). We tend to think that we get things in our own ability, through our jobs, education, or on our own. However, we must know that the seed/money that we have in our hands came from God. We always receive from God first, and when we give, we demonstrate our gratitude for Him through our giving.

In the New Living Translation (NLT), Proverbs 11:24 says, "Give freely and become more wealthy." The world says, "Give freely and become poor. Be stingy and keep everything." It would seem like being stingy would cause you to have more but it does not, you will have less. The Bible continues by saying in verse 25 that "the generous will prosper; those who refresh others will themselves be refreshed." As I meditated on this scripture, I began to wonder, how is it possible to burnout as a Christian? How do you dry up? By refusing to refresh others. Simply start focusing on helping and giving to others, and you'll never go dry. Giving and refreshing others, while focusing on God's people and not on things, will keep you refreshed.

1 John 2:15: *15Love not the world, neither the things that are in the world. If any man love the world, the love of the Father is not in him.*

God knows if you love something, you will support it. You show me somebody or something that you love and I can follow your money to confirm whether or not that is true. You can tell when somebody loves cars, just follow the money trail. You can tell when somebody loves clothes, just follow the money trail. You can tell when somebody loves their wife, child, church or pastor, just follow the money trail.

Matthew 6:19-25: *19Lay not up for yourselves treasures upon earth, where moth and rust doth corrupt, and where thieves break through and steal: 20But lay up for yourselves treasures in heaven, where neither moth nor rust doth corrupt, and where thieves do not break through nor steal: [21]For where your treasure is, there will your heart be also. [22]The light of the body is the eye: if therefore thine eye be single, thy whole body shall be full of light. [23]But if thine eye be evil, thy whole body shall be full of darkness. If therefore the light that is in thee be darkness, how great is that darkness. [24]No man can serve two masters: for either he will hate the one, and love the other; or else he will hold to the one, and despise the other. Ye cannot serve God and mammon. [25]Therefore I say unto you, Take no thought for your life, what ye shall eat, or what ye shall drink; nor yet for your body, what ye shall put on. Is not the life more than meat, and the body than raiment?*

Your hand is an extension of your heart. We must get the revelation that God is on our side and He is able to make all grace abound toward us. When you give in obedience to God's will, His grace is released to you. He will make sure that you never go without, similar to the department store that doesn't tolerate empty shelves. Anytime someone makes a purchase and an item is scanned, the computer sends a message to the distribution center so they can automatically send a replacement for the item that was taken off the shelf so they never run out. That's similar to how God's process works. You never run out of money with God because when you give, it sends a message to heaven that says, 'they just released, give it back, plus some.' God gives it back to you good measure, pressed down, shaken together and running over.

Notice from Matthew 6:19-25, the devil wants you to rely upon earthly treasures (so that) he can steal from you. God says to lay up our treasures in heaven where they will last, where thieves won't break through and steal; for where your treasure is, there will your heart be also. No man can serve two masters, for that he will hate the one and love the other. You can't serve God and mammon.

Mammon is the god of riches, material wealth, and greed. If you listen to the spirit of mammon that's on money, you will be confused. It tries to replace God with things. It promises you security, freedom, power, love, joy, happiness, and the answer to your problems—things that you can only receive from God. The enemy gets access to the hearts of people through and by words. Spirits ride on words. They start telling you that you need more money to live. I've seen people steal money the devil told them to take believing they could get away with it. When they got caught, he was nowhere around.

Your money will definitely talk to you. There was a time at a restaurant that my money was telling me what I could and couldn't buy. Upon arriving at the restaurant, I realized that I didn't have my wallet and heard, 'Dewayne, have you checked your pockets?' Good thing I did, since I had less money than I thought. Because of this, I made my selection by reading the menu from right to left (get it? - by looking at the prices first). Though I wanted a steak, I had to settle for chicken because my money was telling me that I couldn't have steak.

You may be experiencing a situation where your money is telling you that you can't afford to tithe or give. But it's important to seek first God's way of doing things, otherwise, the spirit of mammon will tell you what to do.

Matthew 6:34 tells us to take no thought for tomorrow because tomorrow will take care of itself. We know the thoughts about tomorrow aren't coming from God, because Jesus would have never told us not to take a thought that was coming from God. Mammon/Money will begin to ask 'how you are going to go to school?' 'how are you going to do this or that?' Now those thoughts have to be coming from mammon because we just read where Jesus said that you don't have to take thought about the things in your tomorrow or your future.

When you get money, put God first by paying your tithes and giving offerings. Trust in the Lord with all your heart and lean not to your understanding. In all your ways acknowledge Him and He shall direct your path (Proverbs 3:5-6).

Can you imagine the little woman in the Bible who gave her two mites? Nobody knew that we would be reading about this woman thousands of years later. Jesus was right there watching while all the big givers were giving, yet He talked about this one woman. Do you know why? She gave from her heart, right where she was. No matter where you are in life, if you sow right, God will meet your needs.

As a Christian, it doesn't make a difference how much money you have in your pocket or purse. Your money doesn't make you; you make it. Money makes you more of who you are. If there is an area in your life that is dry, examine it carefully. It can be an indication of what is lacking in your life. If your relationships are dry, give more of yourself to your spouse and/or children. If you don't have friends, show yourself friendly. If your finances are dry, give more money. Many of our financial needs are left unmet because we refuse to keep God first. Instead, we rob Him of blessing us because we want to do it our way and not His way.

Malachi 3:8-11:

8Will a man rob God? Yet ye have robbed me. But ye say, Wherein have we robbed thee? In tithes and offerings. 9Ye are cursed with a curse: for ye have robbed me, even this whole nation. 10Bring ye all the tithes into the storehouse, that there may be meat in mine house, and prove me now herewith, saith the Lord of hosts, if I will not open you the windows of heaven, and pour you out a blessing, that there shall not be room enough to receive it. 11And I will rebuke the devourer for your sakes, and he shall not destroy the fruits of your ground; neither shall your vine cast her fruit before the time in the field, saith the Lord of hosts.

There have been major discussions about whether or not tithing is for today. The Word of God is timeless and never changes. This scripture was written specifically for those who had stopped tithing. God wanted them to return to Him, so they could stand under an open heaven; the place where His blessing would flow to them. To do so, they had to get back into the flow of giving and receiving, and it all started with the tithe.

As Christians, we know that all of our increase comes from God. Why wouldn't we give Him the 10 percent that belongs to Him? This is only an issue because many of us focus on the money aspect of tithing, when in actuality, tithing is about putting God first in your heart. It is an expression of your gratitude and shows that you realize that what's in your hand was placed there by God. The devil has used this as a point of contention with Christians for many centuries. Abraham paid tithes 430 years before the law was given to show his love and thankfulness to God.

In Genesis 14:17, Abraham won his battle against Chedorlaomer and had many spoils. As he returned home, Melchizedek, the king of Salem, and the King of Sodom both came out to meet him. Although Abraham was excited about having won the battle, he knew that he couldn't have won without God, so he offered a tithe to Melchizedek. The King of Sodom told Abraham that he shouldn't do that; that he should only turn over the people, which was his legal right. Abraham refused to keep anything, saying that all of the spoils belonged to God. When you really love someone, no one has to tell you how to express it. The devil tells us the same thing, 'keep your money because you're going to need it.'

The Spirit of God told me to look more closely at the King of Sodom. The name Sodom means to burn with intense heat, to scorch or a place near the Dead Sea. (The Dead Sea has only one opening to receive from the other waterways, compared to the Red Sea, which has two openings to give and receive. Notice, nothing lives in the Dead Sea, yet vegetation and animals thrive in the Red Sea.) When Abraham got the spoils from the battle and it was time to decide what to do, Melchizedek represented Jesus and the King of Sodom represented the devil. Following Melchizedek, Abraham would pay the tithe and continue in God's plan for increase for his life. Had he followed the King of Sodom, he would have ended the blessings of God and ended up in a dead place.

Today, we are faced with making similar decisions. We must determine whether we are going to trust God and watch Him increase us, or listen to the devil and watch our finances dry up. Whatever your current situation, you can give your way into increase.

At popular sporting events, they have their own tithe and offering system, they just don't call it that. The amount of your tithe/ticket will determine where you sit. If your tithes are low, you'll sit in the nosebleed seats. If your tithes are high, you'll sit closer to the field or court. In the church, they let you sit anywhere you choose. You can be a non-tither sitting beside a tither. At the game, we know how much tithes everyone paid. As a matter of fact, they have ushers who want to see your 'tithing record' (ticket) before escorting you to your seat. When the usher gets your tithing record, he or she will direct you to your seat based on the amount you paid. At the game, they want you to pay your tithe before you come in; they don't trust you.

At church, you can come in, take your seat and let the offering bucket pass you by and no one would be any wiser. At the game, the ushers walk around several times asking for an offering by saying, "popcorn, candy and peanuts." Nobody at the game is saying, 'all you want is my money.' People give willingly. We spend large amounts of money at sporting events and on other temporary things, and the devil won't say a word as long as we don't put that money into God's system for increase. Most people think prosperity starts with money, but it doesn't. It starts with God.

Genesis 39:21, 23:

21But the Lord was with Joseph, and shewed him mercy, and gave him favour in the sight of the keeper of the prison. 23The keeper of the prison looked not to anything that was under his hand; because the Lord was with him and that which he did, the Lord made it to prosper.

When Joseph went to jail, he didn't take any cash or his debit card. He couldn't even wear his own clothes. In prison, financially, everyone is at the same place. Joseph had no money, yet the Lord favored Joseph and caused him to prosper. As the Lord was with Joseph, He is with us, giving us favor.

You may be in a financial prison, like Joseph. But just as God was with Joseph, He is with you and He has given you favor. Keep your heart right and obey His

Word, and He will give the desires of your heart—that is to tithe and give offerings.

Here are some steps to assist you in starting or getting back on track with paying your tithes and giving your offerings:

(1) Repent. Change your thinking and way of doing things.

(2) Stop spending. Just like when you're losing weight, you have to stop eating the things that cause you to gain weight. When you see yourself as a person who tithes and gives offerings, you must stop needlessly spending.

Hebrews 12:1-2 reads:

[1]Wherefore seeing we also are compassed about with so great a cloud of witnesses, let us lay aside every weight (spending), and the sin which doth so easily beset us, and let us run with patience the race that is set before us, [2]Looking unto Jesus the author and finisher of our faith; who for the joy that was set before him endured the cross, despising the shame,

and is set down at the right hand of the throne of God.

(3) Make Sacrifices. Sacrifice means to kill, put to death (i.e. the bad habits that prevent you from seeing, submitting, serving, and sowing right).

1 Samuel 15:22:

²²And Samuel said, Hath the Lord as great delight in burnt offerings and sacrifices, as in obeying the voice of the Lord? Behold, to obey is better than sacrifice, and to hearken than the fat of rams.

Yes, to obey (obedience) is better than sacrifice. But, sacrifice will assist you in getting back into obedience. For example, this means every contract that can be legally terminated without affecting your credit must be canceled (be sacrificed). You can turn off the cable TV and cell phones, stop eating out and quit spending money on entertainment, sports packages and season tickets; sell some things that you are no longer using, and use that money toward getting back on track with your tithes and offerings.

(4) Prepare a budget. Preparing a budget will help you

to get things in order so that you can properly allocate and negotiate with your creditors.

Habakkuk 2:2:

²And the Lord answered me, and said, Write the vision, and make it plain upon tables, that he may run that   readeth   it.

Proverbs 20:18:

¹⁸Every purpose is established by counsel: and with good advice make war.

(5) Call Your Creditors. If you are in debt, it is important to call your creditors to negotiate lower payments. Don't allow yourself to become weary if you are told no; simply ask for the next person in management. Confirm that the creditors have accepted the amount you agreed upon in your conversation, and then follow through on your commitment.

Luke 12:58:

⁵⁸When thou goest with thine adversary to the magistrate, as thou art in the way, give diligence that thou mayest be delivered from him; lest he hale thee to

the judge, and the judge deliver thee to the officer, and
the officer cast thee into prison.

(6) Decision-Making Time. After you have followed the
above steps and find that you are still falling short,
then it's time to make a decision. Somebody is going to
get robbed. Will it be God or the creditor? While I can't
tell you what to do, if it was my decision, I would
choose to rob the creditor since Acts 4:19 says, 'I'd
rather obey God than man.'

Acts 4:19-20:

[19]*"But Peter and John answered and said unto*
them, Whether it be right in the sight of God to hearken
unto you (man) more than unto God, judge ye. [20]*For*
we cannot but speak the things which we have seen
and heard."

Deuteronomy 30:19 reads, I call heaven and earth to
record this day against you, that I have set before you
life and death, blessing and cursing: therefore choose
life, that both thou and thy seed may live. Remember,
sowing right isn't just about giving your money. It's
about giving of all of your resources. God wants to

increase you and your giving. The 4 S's of Committed Leadership work. If you see right, you will submit right. If you submit right, you will serve right. If you serve right, you will sow right and become a committed leader.

A KEY TO REMEMBER

Your hand is an extension of your heart.

It is through the giving of our resources that we express our love to others.

QUESTIONS FOR PERSONAL GROWTH

Do you consider yourself a giver? _____

_____

_____

_____

_____

_____

_____

Are you a consistent giver or are you an emotional giver? _____

_____

_____

_____

_____

_____

Do you allow others or circumstances to stop you

from giving? If so, why? _____

_____

_____

What standard or motivation do you use in your

giving? _____

_____

_____

_____

What will you do to sow right or increase your

giving this year?_____

_____

_____

_____

_____

_____

NOTES

ABOUT THE AUTHOR

Dewayne R. Freeman is the Assistant Pastor of Spirit of Faith Christian Center where his brother Michael A. Freeman is the Pastor. "Pastor Dewayne," as he is affectionately known, is an awesome uncompromising teacher of God's Word. He  teaches with a powerful anointing, yet with simplicity and practical examples to assist those who hear to receive revelation of God's Word. He believes that faith is simply acting on the Word of God and that it is the key to unlocking the door of victory in the life of every believer. Assistant Pastor Dewayne is an example of a faithful man. His faithfulness is demonstrated through his support to his pastor and service as the Assistant Pastor, Director of Ministry of Helps and overseer of the Bible Studies Programs at Spirit of Faith Christian Center. He has been married to his beautiful wife Anjelisa (Lisa) Freeman for over twenty-eight years. He attributes the success of his marriage to his commitment and obedience to God's Word. He believes that both commitment and obedience to the things of God have brought an anointing on his life that guarantees success in every area of his life.

Other Books by Dewayne Freeman...

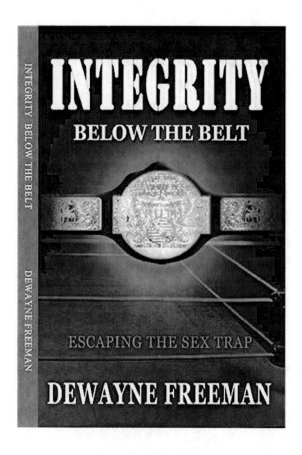

Visit **www.DewayneFreemanMinistries.com**
to get your copy!

CPSIA information can be obtained at www.ICGtesting.com
Printed in the USA
LVOW12s1940080515

437756LV00004B/4/P